# AS THE VALLEY WAS

A pictorial view of the community life in the Yakima River Valley from the Yakima River's origin at Cle Elum to its junction with the Columbia River during the era 1900-1915.

---

*Compiled and edited by Jeanne R. Crawford*

*Executive Editor, Kay Kime*

Cover Painting by Phil Kooser

---

Publications by Yakima Valley Museum

Printed by Shields Bag and Printing Co.

# ACKNOWLEDGEMENTS

The photographs taken by Frank Lanterman of the Yakima scene over a period of many years have basically made this book possible. Prints of his negatives were made by Jack Whitnall. The first edition was published by Yakima Federal Savings and Loan as a public service, and a second edition was published by the Yakima Valley Society for the Preservation of Early Western Americana (the Frontier Museum).

Additional pictures of Yakima and all pictures of other areas have been lent by generous associations and individuals, and many other persons have contributed their help, encouragement and historical knowledge to the pages of this book.

Grateful thanks go to George M. Martin; Mrs. Claude E. Smith and the Yakima Valley Museum and Historical Association; George F. Beck; the Yakima Dailies; Mrs. June Thurston, Yakima Valley Regional Librarian, and her entire staff, especially Ross Carter, Mrs. Hazel Nelson and Miss Dolores Plath; Edward Nolan; Louis F. Janeck of Northridge, California; Porter Lombard; the First Baptist Church; Mrs. A. E. Rasmussen and the First Christian Church; O. E. Brashears; St. Michael's Episcopal Church; Mrs. Mary F. Kirby, Marquette High School; W. A. McKenzie of the Northern Pacific Railway, Minneapolis, Minnesota; Mrs. Norman Gossett; Mrs. Marie Donelson, City of Yakima; Richard Landis, Yakima Fire Department; Mrs. George T. Corbett.

And to the Wapato Pioneer Association, Mrs. George Hanson; the Mary L. Goodrich Public Library, Toppenish, and Mrs. Iris Dahlman; Mrs. Alpha Piland, Mrs. Lois Gelhart and Miss Alice Beutel, Granger; Roscoe Sheller, Sunnyside; the Sunnyside Pioneer Association and Mrs. Claude Beck; the Grandview Historical Association and Mrs. E. H. Richards of the Bleyhl Community Library, Grandview; the Benton County Museum and Historical Society and Clarence Dykes, Prosser; Harry Fisher, Prosser; the Tri-City Herald; Mrs. Fred Story, Mabton.

And to Mrs. Roy Haines, Zillah; Albert Schober, Cle Elum; Kittitas County Historical Society and Miss Clareta Olmstead Smith and Miss Leta Smith; Oliver Mountjoy and Arthur Gregory of the Ellensburg Fire Department; Fred Breckon, all of Ellensburg; Robert Lince of Selah; Mrs. Russell J. Thompson and John Thompson of Naches.

For his exceptional interest in the old photographs and his hours of work to reproduce them for this book, a special accolade to Harry H. Krueger of Shields Bag and Printing Co.

And last but by no means least, a loving and grateful acknowledgement to Mrs. Lena Lanterman, whose alert mind and refreshing reminiscences at the age of 85 did so much to bring alive the Yakima her husband so loved and faithfully recorded.

—The Editor.

# FOREWORD

The Yakima Valley Museum & Historical Association is pleased to acknowledge the generosity of the Yakima Federal Savings & Loan Association and the Yakima Valley Society for the Preservation of Early Western Americana in transferring to the Museum all rights to this pictorial essay of the Yakima Valley and we are proud to publish this Museum edition for the pleasure of all of the people.

**As The Valley Was** is one of a series of historical publications which will be made available from time to time.

Yakima - May, 1976 — George M. Martin
President
Yakima Valley Museum
& Historical Assn.

Cle Elum, looking southwest, circa 1911-1912.

Looking southeast, Cle Elum, 1911-1912.

# The river rises in CLE ELUM

View of Cle Elum, looking south.

Early day July 4 parade in Cle Elum.

Hotel in Cle Elum.

Cle Elum High School,
built 1904.

Coal bunkers, west of Northern Pacific depot, 1910.

Steam Laundry, Cle Elum, circa 1911.

Roslyn after big snow in January, 1913.

Matt Kauzlarich owned this building
on East First Street, 1916.

# ELLENSBURG

Ellensburg, founded earlier than other towns along the Yakima River, was a settled community by the early 1900s, its local historical climax having come in 1889 when much of the town was destroyed by a great fire. But the citizens rebuilt the community, originally settled in 1867 and named by John Shoudy after his wife, Ellen. This early view of Ellensburg is from the Normal School, toward the west.

Pearl Street, around the turn of the century.

The Ellensburg fire department's steam pumper.

Post office was on North Pearl near Fifth Avenue, in 1903. Oliver Hinman, second from left, was postmaster.

Interior, Ellensburg Saloon.

Moore's Lodging House offered rooms for 25 and 50 cents.

Built in 1890, Horton Hotel became Antlers Hotel in 1900.

Interior of Turner's printing shop.

R. A. Turner published The Dawn twice weekly here.

Bank of Ellensburg interior.

Toby and Nancy, Ellensburg's Indian couple.

Washington National Bank was rebuilt after 1889 fire. This 1888 photo shows the city's first horse show.

**Gilmour and Gilmour Grocery, 1910.**

**Interior, Gilmour Grocery in
Cadwell Building, 1912.**

The Farmers Bank, built 1911.

Pearson Block, Fourth Avenue and Main, built 1908.

Fourth Avenue between Pine and Pearl, circa 1910.

Early Ellensburg business area.

Olmstead cabin, built 1875.

Kittitas County courthouse, Ellensburg.

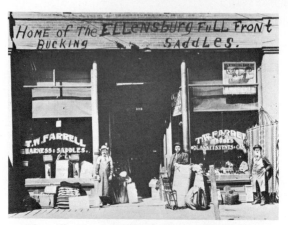

Farrell's Harness, Saddle Shop, Main Street.

Interior of Farrell's shop.

Northern Pacific depot in Ellensburg.

Patenaude orchard near Ellensburg, 1908.

Baling hay, Kittitas County, early 1900s.

Cascade Irrigation Canal near Ellensburg.

Sheep shearing at Hamilton's ranch near Ellensburg.

First Christian Church.

Crowd, right, hears President Theodore Roosevelt, 1903; below, welcome arch for the President's visit.

Washington Elementary School.

First Presbyterian Church.

Ellensburg Normal School.

# NACHES

Naches' early Case Hotel.

Dimmick's livery stable.

The Naches School after building was enlarged.

The plat for the town of Naches was filed in 1906.
An early panorama shows the school, early church.

The Naches depot, 1907.

# SELAH

This stone bank marked the intersection of East Naches Avenue and the Wenas Road in Selah. Early business buildings along the main street, circa 1911, were frame structures.

Selah's first trading post, this store later became the Anchor Store.

Selah Central School, built 1911.

Another view of the main business block, 1909.

King's Hall had upstairs meeting room, downstairs blacksmith shop. First post office was in house at left.

Hotel Selah, rebuilt after 1908 fire.

Swedish Mission Church, right, and Methodist Church, circa 1911.

The main street from the intersection where the Anchor Store stood.

Selah Valley looking north, prior to 1913.

The main street, later Naches Avenue, looking toward Anchor Store, which was in the middle of the crossing.

Looking toward Selah from the hill, after 1911.

# YAKIMA

In 1905, in the era in which this photograph was taken, North Yakima was not yet twenty years old. The town had been located by the Northern Pacific Railway on a site deemed more adequate for expansion than the original city of Yakima (now Union Gap or Old Town). The city was growing from a typical frontier town with frame buildings and plank sidewalks into a community whose farsighted downtown property owners were constructing more permanent buildings, and whose civic and business leaders would debate the question of street paving for several years. By 1905, a United States President had visited the little town, its main avenue was stretching to the east and west, and in the next few years buildings that still stand would be erected.

A beautiful depot, designed by Cass Gilbert, architect of the Minnesota State Capitol, was the first stop of hundreds who came to join in the land boom of the era. O. A. Fechter, president of the Yakima Valley Bank, described the entrance to North Yakima, opposite: "A cement platform, 900 feet long . . . your first glance rests on a grassy park in which a fountain is playing and in which trees cast grateful shade . . . the Northern Pacific Railway station is unique in design and one of the most attractive on the line."

The newcomer to North Yakima who strolled from the depot to the corner of Yakima Avenue and Front Street saw this perspective of the avenue toward the east. Far left is the Lund Building, built in 1899; far right, the business block which Frank Shardlow, orchardist and hop grower, erected in 1902, with his Red Onion Saloon on the ground floor.

This is the street that became a sea of mud after each rain, prompting concern by civic and business leaders and this comment by the North Yakima Republic in January, 1906: "The present condition of the avenue is calling forth more discreditable remarks from visitors to the city than anything else in the whole Yakima country. Mud on the avenue is as bad as it is on any highway in the valley and there is now no relief." Although businessmen, many of whom owned several lots, were willing to bear part of the cost of paving, two years dragged by before the city council approved Ordinance 591 in February 1908 for the "improvement of Yakima Avenue." Part of the opposition came from one councilman who said, "I do not believe in going head over heels in debt for such a luxury. . . . What we owe is more a discredit to us than the mud."

YAKIMA AVE. E. FROM 1ST ST.

Yakima Avenue east from First Street shows old
flat-roofed Miller Building at Second Street corner.

Yakima Avenue east from Front Street, circa 1902.

A third horse was added to the fire department team in 1907.

Flags and flowers bedecked fire department equipment on Independence Day, 1904, when wagon and pumper were rolled out along Front Street. In 1906 when C. M. Hauser was fire chief, the department demonstrated its speed for Everett's visiting mayor and fire chief. "In 40 seconds from the time the alarm was sounded the big grey team thundered around the corner of Front and Yakima Avenue; in 50 seconds they had crossed First Street; in 70 seconds the fire team had passed the Second Street crossing and in just 2:44 the hose had been connected with the hydrant at the corner of Yakima and Third Street." Although impressed, the visiting firemen said they could do it faster!

By the turn of the century, the 300-seat Switzer's Opera House, built in 1889 across from the depot grounds, had become a brewery. City offices adjoined it on the north.

RDS-EYE VIEW N-E. FROM CITY HALL.

This is the view from the city hall looking west across the tracks, just after the turn of the century. Depot park is immediately in foreground.

Larson's Theatre on the northwest corner of Second Street and A Street, and the courthouse, north of it in the same block, dominated this view from the city hall on Front Street.

North Yakima's original station was built in 1885.

Built in 1898, this depot designed by Cass Gilbert stood until 1910, when it was sold for $100, moved and converted into apartments.

A shady park adjoining the depot was a popular spot.

The new Northern Pacific depot, north of the former site, was completed in May, 1910.

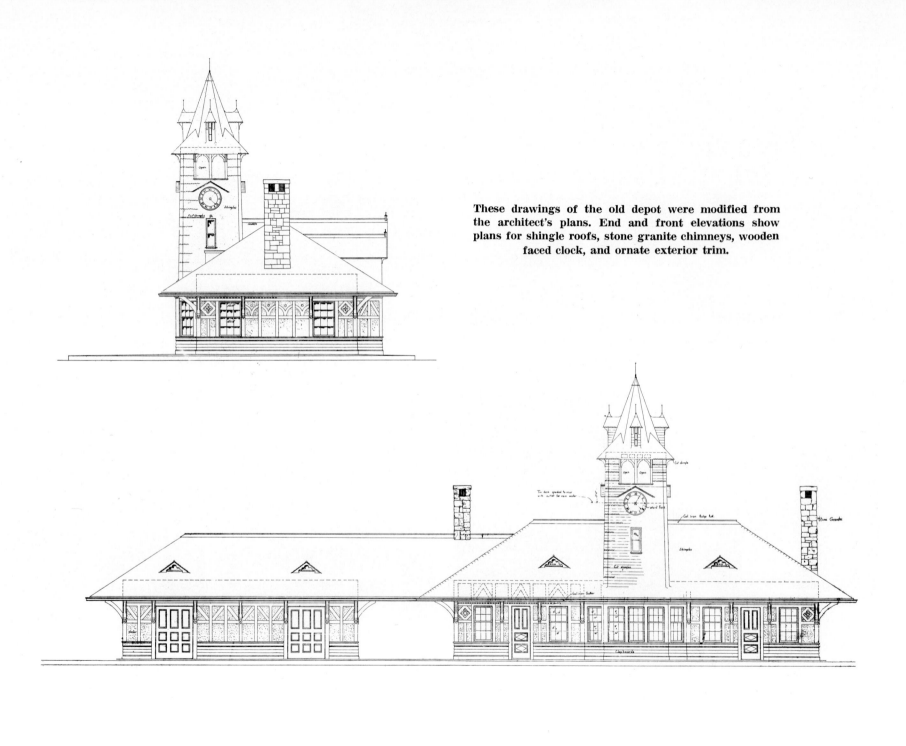

These drawings of the old depot were modified from the architect's plans. End and front elevations show plans for shingle roofs, stone granite chimneys, wooden faced clock, and ornate exterior trim.

Summertime in North Yakima meant the excitement of Ringling Brothers Circus which came almost every year with its exciting animals, blaring bands, pretty girls and other traditional circus acts.

Elephants line up for a parade, near the depot.

Ringling carriages are unloaded at North Yakima depot.

Horses parade on East Yakima Avenue near Third Street.

Water wheels were early-day irrigation aids.

Well-drilling machine for Congdon's orchards.

Congdon's Artesian well comes in!

Yakima Avenue east from Front Street, circa 1903. Schott's Cash Store later became part of four-story Washington Hotel. Twenty-year old frame buildings on south side of street burned in May 1906, shortly after city council had voted against removing them. Paper had noted that "when these buildings are torn or burned down the last of the early day shacks will have been removed from the avenue."

1905 pack train against background of north side of avenue, between First and Second Streets.

Board walks border Yakima Avenue between Third and Fourth Streets, 1902.

Yakima Tea Co. in 1904-1905 was at 118 East Yakima Avenue, present site of Yakima Federal Savings and Loan Association.

Yakima Avenue looking toward Second Street. S. O. Hawkes and Son, Lee Semon Men's Wear, now occupy corner and adjacent buildings.

First National Bank, southwest corner of Yakima Avenue and Second Street, now site of Larson Building.

Closer view of corner shows old flat-topped Miller Building, new Ditter Building, right.

Cahalan and Co. at 218 East Yakima Avenue later moved to new Miller Building.

The Syndicate Building, circa 1900. In later years building was enlarged, third story removed. Now Larson-Andrews Building.

Indians rest along South Second Street.

In downtown North Yakima.

Chestnut Street strollers.

A family group in town.

Indians pass Yakima Valley Bank, Yakima and First Street.

"Suzie", famed Indian character.

Frank Lanterman posed this, called it "Squaws".

Mother and baby.

A. E. Larson opened this $15,000 theatre, familiarly known as the opera house, on June 11, 1900, with a stage show, Evil Eye. The theatre had a sloping floor, seated 1050, and was lighted by 450 incandescent lamps. Youngsters sneaked to the balcony by the outside stairway. In 1907, Larson's Theatre, at Second and A Streets, was sold to John Cort who renamed it the Yakima.

William Jennings Bryan, on March 31, 1900, spoke "under the lofty walls of the new auditorium", Larson's Theatre. Dissension over his coming visit had been noted by the weekly Republic which reported argument about where he should stay while in North Yakima. Although invited to a large private home, he should stay at a hotel, said some, "where the common people can find him and pay their respects." Unfriendly to Bryan, the newspaper predicted that those who would "compose the Bryan crowd will expect to hear a speech the like of which has never fallen from the lips of man in this valley" but added that he would be "just a voice, talking for himself." "Orator Bryan Speaks . . . a Crowd of 4000 People Listens to a Rehash of Familiar Fallacies . . . His Own Followers Fear that his Magnetism and Power are Things of the Past." Under this several-deck headline after his visit it was recorded that the audience "listened with patience to his mellifluous harangue and saved their applause."

Mr. and Mrs. Lanterman's home at 610 North Second Street.

One of North Yakima's first two mail carriers, volunteer fireman, musician, amateur photographer, Frank Lanterman recorded Yakima for over 30 years, carefully mounted his pictures in albums, dated and saved his hundreds of negatives. In this book, Yakima is seen mainly through his lens.

Mr. and Mrs. Lanterman in the 1910 Reo owned by friends, Mr. and Mrs. E. G. Peck.

Unveiled (facing page) on July 4, 1902, this monument was "erected in memory of the Fallen of Company E, 1, Wash., U.S. Vol. Inft., 1898-1899." The Red Cross society ordered the memorial fountain, a statue of Col. Weisenberger, an officer much loved by Company E. The unveiling took place at the intersection of Yakima Avenue and Third Street, with the Coffin Building in construction behind it. Much discussion preceded the erection of the statue regarding its location, and each souvenir lucky penny sold to the townspeople gave a vote on its site. The city council opposed the location, finally chosen, as being obstructive to traffic.

The Memorial Fountain dominated Yakima Avenue for several years, but was finally moved to the new courthouse lawn in 1907. Many years later it was moved again to its present position on Naches Parkway.

In August 1903 the Yakima Brass Band sponsored Southern Carnival Co. for several days. At Yakima Avenue and Front Street Harry DuBelle performed on high wire.

Matt Gay's 100 foot dive into four feet of water was carnival hit.

Along South First Street, the stairway ride was popular.

View southeast from Sloan Building (Yakima Avenue and First Street) looks across Chestnut Street toward Central School on South Second Street. Tiny sloping-roof shack, left center, appears as Hose Cart shed in lower right photo. Both lower photos were taken from Chestnut Street, between First and Second. Left one looks east toward corner of Second Street where Fisher Harness and Saddles was opposite Cadwell Building. Lower right looks north through alley toward buildings on Yakima Avenue. Circa 1901.

"Let the residents of North Yakima and the citizens of Yakima county turn out en masse to greet the President as befits his station. Forget the bitter animosities of partisan feeling and let the spirit of united support among Democrats, Republicans, Populists and Socialists alike prevail." So urged the Yakima Herald in anticipation of the visit of President Theodore Roosevelt on May 25, 1903. The president would be "the most noted person" to visit North Yakima since Bryan, the Herald noted, adding that "he does not care to be bored by a reception but instead he prefers to be driven for a short distance around the town and get a view of the far-famed Yakima Valley." Several boxes of choice Yakima apples were presented to the President, and "doubtless struck tender chords in the hearts of all and [were] the cause of many surprising expressions concerning the wonderful results of irrigation."

Official greeters awaited TR's scheduled 10:30 a.m. arrival.

Crowds lined tracks watching for President's train.

The Memorial Fountain was specially decorated for the day.

President's carriage crosses First Street.

The President waves to Yakima Avenue crowds.

Many follow Roosevelt east on Yakima Avenue.

Roosevelt speaks from Naches Parkway stand.

The county courthouse at Second and B Streets had been moved from Old Town in 1886 when the relocation was made to North Yakima. It was festooned with patriotic colors for the President's visit.

Washington State Fair, Yakima, 1904.

Apple display, 1901 State Fair.

Commercial exhibit, 1904 State Fair.

"The Course," Yakima fairgrounds, circa 1900.

Balloon ascension, 1904 State Fair.

1702

Val Gandy, right, had the first car in North Yakima, circa 1904. Vice president of Golden Northwest Fruit and Vegetable Canning Co., he lived here only briefly. Cars were "stabled" like horses of an earlier year, in the photo above of Yakima Automotive Co. interior, probably taken around 1912.

RED MEN'S PARADE
MAY 12 1904

Rarely photographed because of sunlight angle, the south side of Yakima Avenue
is seen from First Street intersection, looking toward Front Street and west side.

Railroad bridge over Naches River, 1901.

Old Selah bridge across
Naches River, 1902.

Freight train crossing old Naches bridge, circa 1902.

Mesatche Mountain, Gold Hill to right.

Pack train carries supplies to miners.

Miners' cabins, Gold Hill.

Prospectors gather before cabin.

Gold Hill ore dump.

The Gold Hill area, near Morse (Moore's) Creek on Chinook Pass, has been mined for many, many years. Placer mining played out in 1900 but prospectors continued to dig, stake claims, incorporate and sell stock. Tom and Bob Fife bought many early claims. Pictures, circa 1900.

North Yakima's first school, Central School, 217 S. 2nd St.,
built in 1888, razed in 1924.

Columbia School, 112 N. 4th Ave., was built in 1890
for high school and elementary classes.

High school, with Lincoln annex for elementary classes, N. 3rd St.,
built in 1900, burned Jan. 6, 1907, last day of Christmas vacation!

From this St. Joseph Academy, first class was graduated in 1903.
This brick structure was kept as wing when building was enlarged.

Mrs. Ella Stair was principal of the high school classes in Central School for many years. She was "dearly loved" by her students to whom she read stories from the myths and classics each morning, and "made them so vivid that the severest disciplinary measure she could employ was the loss of the reading period." Here are two views of her classroom.

Interior of the Lincoln School after 1907 fire.

Only shell remained of Lincoln School after fire.

New Lincoln School on same site was "one of most beautiful and convenient grade buildings on the Coast."

Nob Hill School was way out in the country.

Barge School, completed in 1905, was designed by N. C. Gauntt, also architect for new Lincoln and North Yakima High Schools.

North Yakima High School neared completion in 1908.
Building cost $120,000, was "one of most modern school
buildings in the United States."

The new high school was the "pride of Central Washington," a "handsome structure," with "earnest, con-
scientious, faithful, efficient faculty."

Marquette College, built in 1909, was originally a
grade school, became a high school in 1918.

The new St. Joseph Academy was started in April
1909, dedicated on December 12 in the same year.

THE NP DEPOT

CENTRAL SCHOOL

BAPTIST CHURCH

THE COURTHOUSE

CHRISTIAN CHURCH

The statue stands as a sentinel over snow-covered
Yakima Avenue, circa 1905.

The W. E. Coumbe home, 415 N. 3rd St. Coumbe was
vice president of Eastern Furniture Co.

The 115 N. Naches Avenue home of Ira P. Englehart,
attorney and notary public.

Frank P. Shardlow's home at 402 N. 2nd St. was another show place residence of North Yakima.

A. B. Weed, hop grower, built this home
in 1905 at 307 N. 2nd St.

William F. Wohlstein's home at 806 N. 2nd St.

Henry C. Thede, postal carrier, lived
at 702 N. 2nd St.

C. S. Wright, orchestra director, lived
at 610 N. 4th St.

Wohlstein, a painter, decorated his front room
ceiling with garlands of flowers.

Dining room of Wohlstein's home, like his other
rooms, displayed his artistic talent.

Second Selah bridge across Yakima River, 1911.

Moxee bridge over Yakima River.

Roads wind through Selah Gap.

Union Gap bridge, circa 1901.

Zillah-Toppenish bridge.

Yakima Avenue east from First Street, 1901.

Photos taken a few years apart show change in irrigation ditch along Naches Avenue.

Roof-top vista a few years later shows First Presbyterian Church steeple in foreground, Carnegie Library, Marquette College, St. Joseph's Catholic Church spires.

Wolf's boathouse and landing at Lake Keechelus, early 1900s.

Hike in mountains near Keechelus, 1912.

Camping in woods near Lake Keechelus, 1912.

Camp Fire set mood for families gathered at lake.

Trains never ceased to interest early photographers. They grabbed their cameras at times of arrivals, departures, and wrecks.

Small engine pulled flat cars loaded with material to pave Yakima Avenue, 1908.

Tower of depot and roof of old opera house are background for this steam engine, circa 1907.

This engine was used in Lake Keechelus area. North Yakimans rode the train to the depot at the lake, then boated across to their favorite resorts.

Telephone conduit is laid on North Second Street in early years.

Progress of town to westward included grading Yakima Avenue at Ninth Avenue.

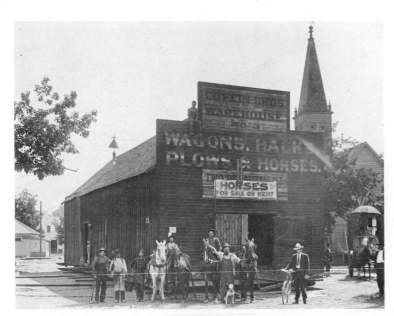

Being moved to make room for the new post office is a Coffin Bros. warehouse. Methodist Church at Second and Chestnut Streets in background.

The Minnesota Building on South Second Street, after its completion, housed Hotel Locke in 1910, following year became Grand Hotel, "strictly modern, city center".

Early Methodist Church at Chestnut and Third Streets cost $6,000 when built in 1891.

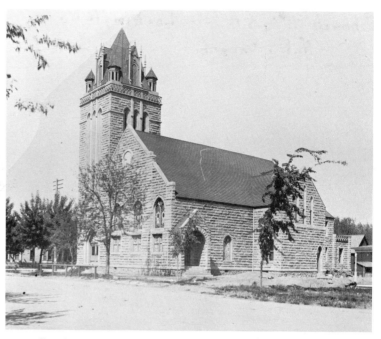

Constructed in 1905, new Methodist Church (which many years later became Stone Church of God) cost $40,000.

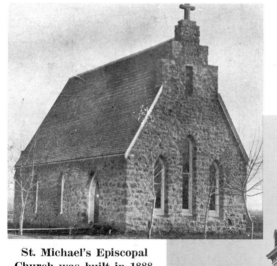

St. Michael's Episcopal Church was built in 1888.

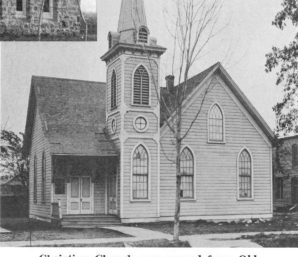

Christian Church was moved from Old Town to North Third Street.

In 1908, new Christian Church was built at Third and B Streets.

Early Presbyterian Church at Fourth
and A Streets was used until 1903.

Cornerstone was laid in July, 1902, for the new Presbyterian Church, southwest corner of Third and A Streets.

Baptist Church, built in 1892 at cost of $4,000, was on
North Fourth Street, between Yakima Avenue and A
Street.

New Baptist Church cornerstone for Yakima Avenue
building was laid May 2, 1908.

Bishop Edward John O'Dea presides at cornerstone ceremony of St. Joseph's Church.

Choir boys leave after May 22, 1903, service.

St. Joseph's Church, built entirely of basalt in style of Roman architecture, is partially finished.

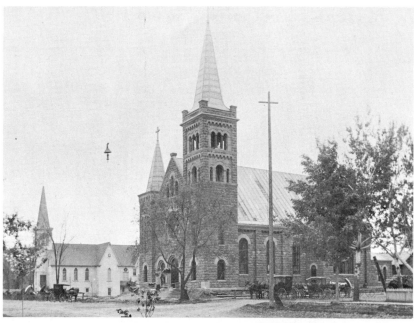

Frame church built in 1888 contrasts with new building, was later torn down to make room for Marquette.

First mass in new church was May 1, 1905. Church was dedicated in January, 1906.

Around 1905, the same intersection was dominated by Coffin and Clogg buildings on north side, fashionable Yakima Hotel on southwest corner.

The Memorial Fountain guards the intersection of Yakima Avenue and Third Street, with Clogg Building behind it.

Early parades drew crowds to downtown North Yakima, provided excitement for townspeople. Right, band marching on North Third Street toward Yakima Avenue passes North Yakima Furniture Co. in Clogg Building. The Presbyterian Church steeple is in the background. Below, Woodmen's Float crosses at Yakima and Second, near first location of Pioneer Drug Co. which was on northwest corner for several years, moved in 1910 to new Miller Building. Right, floats approach Second and Yakima, with Larson's Theatre in background.

Interior of Janeck Drug Store, East Yakima
Avenue.

OPPOSITE PAGE: Bonds for the new county courthouse had already been sold and work was being pushed by Contractor W. W. Felton when the old courthouse burned on May 5, 1906. News of the fire edged the three-day old San Francisco earthquake off the front page of the local paper. Official records were saved by hundreds of helping people, and the building was repaired until the new one could be finished. "The new courthouse will be the most welcome improvement to the city and county that the people have ever had the pleasure of anticipating," it was predicted.

North First Street office of J. H. Needham and
John C. MacCrimmon, real estate salesmen, 1906.

During the fire.

After the fire.

Courthouse, Larson's Theatre on North Second Street.

The cornerstone was laid for new courthouse on June 5, 1906, postponed after proposed Memorial Day ceremony was protested by GAR. More than 1,000 persons attended the "impressive exercises."

The new courthouse, said Attorney Henry Snively at cornerstone-laying, "will give to future generations an idea of the progress of the Yakima county during the present period."

"Enroute to picnic on the Columbia River," Mr. Lanterman labeled the photograph above. The Lantermans, her sister Muriel, her parents Mr. and Mrs. Newman Hutchings and friends rode the train to Beverly, then drove eight miles by wagon to their property on the river for a picnic.

A five-day flood in November 1906 did hundreds of thousands of dollars damage in the valley, undermining the foundations of some bridges, washing out others, and almost cutting the area off from the rest of the world.

Gap in the NPRR grade at
Naches River Bridge.

NY and V bridge at Union Gap.

Washed out Naches River bridge lodged
under NPRR span.

Another view of fallen
North Yakima and Valley bridge.

Selah bridge on Naches River went down.
Ruined vineyards in foreground.

New river channel after flood.

A street scene in Rimrock, Washington.

View up-river from Rimrock bridge.

Sawmill and lumber yard at Rimrock.

Looking down Tieton River from dam site.

Residence street in Rimrock.
(Photos second decade of 1900s.)

Construction of the new Elks Temple was proposed in 1906, a year that promised "more than any year in the past" for growing town.

The drive for funds for the YMCA, finally completed in 1908 on South Fourth Street, started in 1906.

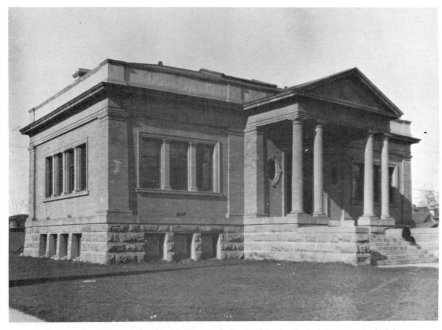

Carnegie Library was dedicated in 1906, to help serve "mighty influx of immigration" to area.

The Federal Building and post office was built in 1911 at Chestnut and Third Streets.

This view of Second Street, looking north from the corner of Chestnut in 1912, shows enlarged Miller Building, with sixth story added also.

North Naches Avenue, circa 1913.

Street car line, North Fourth Street.

First half of Miller Building was completed by Alex Miller in 1907, was the site of the Cahalan Co. until 1912. Henry Cahalan was president, John J. Callahan vice-president.

Yakima Avenue was paved in 1908, as were numbered streets north and south for two or three blocks.

**Hop picking at North Yakima.**

**Elegant young visitor calls on her family.**

**Group poses after successful season.**

**Sacks of hops are loaded at Morriers'.**

Filling hop sacks.

Tent city at Morriers' hop ranch near Moxee, 1913.

North Yakima family's tent home during hop season. Family groups virtually moved to Moxee during the fall hop season, spent two or three weeks there. Other members of the family came to visit during the harvest.

Family group picking hops.

**Country barnyard near Yakima, circa 1915.**

**Schoonover Ranch near Naches.**

**Horseshoe bend of Naches River.**

**Naches Valley from Rowe Hill.**

**Sunnyside Dam.**

**Fort Simcoe blockhouse.**

**Ahtanum Mission.**

**Ahtanum Narrows.**

Spraying fruit trees, North Yakima, circa 1901.

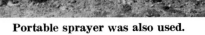

Portable sprayer was also used.

Four-year old apple orchard, North Yakima.

**Stone Horticultural Building was built in 1907.**

The Cascade Lumber Company was incorporated in 1902, and purchased as its first property land known as the Lewis Ranch, where the mill was built. Log ponds were made, right and below, by digging and making embankments. Water for them was secured through a flume from the Yakima River, excavated at the same time. The first sawmill started operations in 1903. Until 1916, all logs were driven from timber country down the Yakima River, into a dam at Pomona, from where they were sluiced in small amounts six miles downriver. The logs were diverted into the flume, then into the ponds, a precarious undertaking because of the rise and fall of the river.

Pulling in logs in Cascade flume.

Yakima River at sawmill.

Boom used to corral logs, second Selah bridge in background.

Log in flume. Before days of cars, sawmill was easily accessible place of interest to visit.

Inlet for mill pond. Selah bridge in background, 1911.

Cascade Mill log pond.

Early saw mill.

Driving logs in mill pond and ditch.

Orchards west of Yakima, 1905.

Picking hops
in early days.

Looking toward town from Nob Hill.

Grape harvest at Huxtable house "out in the
country" at Barge and 24th Avenue.

Naches Gap is in the distance in this picture looking across Yakima Avenue. House at left stands
at 1911 W. Yakima Avenue.

Packing peaches at the Van Payton ranch, 1900.

Interior of fruit warehouse, turn of the century.

Contrasting with the second photo in the Yakima pages is this view of the Avenue in 1908, showing the changes of only a few years. Stone and brick structures rise to two and three stories, the street has been recently paved with vitrified brick, and street cars provide public transportation.

Another president of the United States visited North Yakima on Sept. 29, 1909, William Howard Taft, whose stop here was part of a 57-day tour through 35 states and territories. His schedule was closely timed, from his arrival at 5:30 a.m. to his departure for Seattle at 2 p.m. Handshaking had been ruled out by the time he reached North Yakima, as he was too tired, but at the reception which followed his speech he was greeted by 70 persons per minute, faster than the record of 60 per minute in other cities!

President Taft originally was scheduled to speak in Naches Parkway where President Roosevelt had appeared six years before, but the new courthouse was finally decided upon, as it would give protection in case of windy weather. "The building would act as a shield for the nation's chief executive," would be a sounding board and the lawns would provide more space for the crowds.

For the presidential parade, thirteen cars were listed, the first eleven for members of the official party and dignitaries, the other two "for emergency." "So impressed with the orderliness of the city were the president's guard and aides that no secret service men watched the chief executive of the nation here," and went ahead to prepare for his next stop, the newspaper recounted.

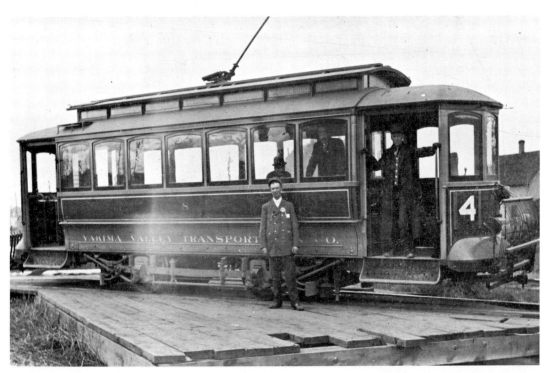

Interurban lines operated by the Yakima Valley Transportation Co. with freight cars like this included Fruitvale, Wiley City, Selah, Harwood and Orchard. Otto Piske was its motorman.

Although financial problems arose shortly after formation of a company to serve North Yakima and the surrounding area with an electric railway, eventually many miles of track were laid through the city and to the suburbs. This car operated by Eugene Campfield served one of the intown routes, which in the second decade of the century included Fairview, Maple Street, Cascade Mill, Fourth Street and Nob Hill.

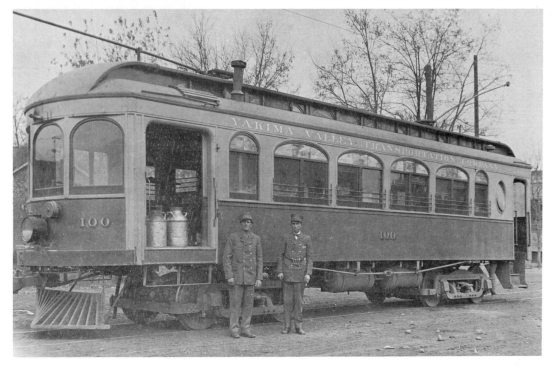

Under construction in 1907 and 1908 was the North Coast Railroad, later to be known as the Oregon-Washington Railroad and Navigation Company, and eventually to become part of the Union Pacific. On March 22, 1911, completion of the line and all of its depots was celebrated by an excursion from Walla Walla to North Yakima, with stops all along the route.

North Coast track-laying machinery.

Arrival of first North Coast train in North Yakima.

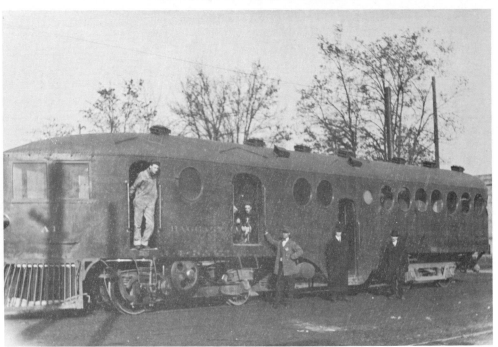

North Coast Railroad gasoline motor car.

Nearing completion in September, 1911, was the Masonic Temple at Yakima Avenue and Fourth Street. Below, ground had been broken on September 10, 1910, with many Masonic dignitaries participating in the ceremony.

Masonic Temple groundbreaking. Partly finished Commercial Hotel behind barricade, YMCA left rear.

John J. Callahan, who had been in business with Harry Cahalan, opened his own store in the Masonic Temple a year or two after it was completed.

**The Yakima resident who stopped at the corner of the Avenue and Fourth Street
in 1914 and 1915 saw this heart of the downtown as he looked westward.**

1156 - Third Street, North Yakima Washington.

Although the postcard said "Third Street" this is Second Street looking south in 1912 from midway between Yakima Avenue and A Street. Miller Building dominates view with Central School in distance, right.

East from Front Street in 1908 or 1909, this view of more permanent buildings recalls earlier frame structures that lined a dustier road just a few years earlier.

No. 3, YAKIMA AVE. EAST, NORTH YAKIMA, WASHINGTON.

In April 1912 the second annual Blossom Festival was held, with a parade starting the three-day program. Officials' automobiles drove slowly up the crowd-lined avenue.

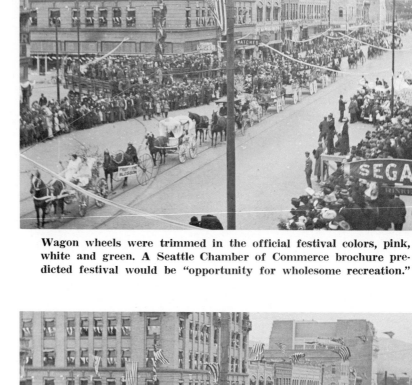

Wagon wheels were trimmed in the official festival colors, pink, white and green. A Seattle Chamber of Commerce brochure predicted festival would be "opportunity for wholesome recreation."

Moose float in the parade. Festival also featured a cantata, "Rose Maiden", by North Yakima Choral Society; dances; sightseeing trips on electric cars; "general jollification" on the final evening.

Veterans' group marches. Festival was a success, would continue each year to draw people to North Yakima to see the great orchard area, "almost one mass of fragrant blossoms".

First prize auto, 1913 parade.

Ditter Brothers float.

Children's dog teams are parade unit.

Sisto Granger is crowned 1913 Blossom Festival Queen, by Mayor Jack Splawn.

Zillah Band marches.

Elks float, 1913 festival parade.

**Fire department, 1913 Blossom Festival parade.**

**Fruitvale Come and Help Club entry.**

**Commercial floats participated, too.**

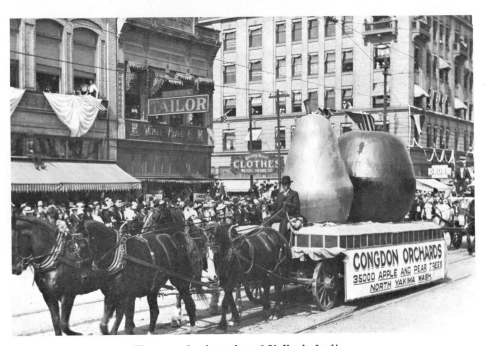

**Float emphasizes size of Valley's fruit.**

The queen and her court rode on this float in the 1913 Blossom Festival parade. Several towns in the Valley nominated their prettiest girls as queen candidates.

City officials ride in style in 1913 parade!

**Mt. Rainier from a suburban vista point.**

**Mt. Adams, from the Fourth Street bridge.**

The Commercial Hotel, circa 1913. Wilson Building on corner had been built in 1902, was location of Kauffman Millinery for many years.

The Avenue, bedecked for a holiday, 1916.

Fire Dep't. Headquarters, North Yakima, Wash.

In 1913 the North Yakima Fire Department moved to its new headquarters after many years in the old Front Street location by city hall.

In 1912 the department became only completely motorized one west
of the Mississippi, included a 75-foot aerial ladder in its equipment.

This Webb Motor fire engine was unit of North Yakima fire-fight
ing apparatus. These pictures were taken in 1914.

In front of Fire Station No. 2 on North Fourth Avenue this com-
bination chemical rig and steamer were pictured.

Although in the early days North Yakima fire fighters were volunteers and funded their department with balls, dances, and other social functions, lack of concern by the city council finally permeated the firemen's ranks and they resigned in a group in 1904, spending $35 for a final dinner and dividing up the balance of the department's monies among the men. The department was re-organized on a volunteer basis but not successfully, and in 1905 a new North Yakima Fire Department came into existence with five paid men and ten volunteers.

Early Helliesen Lumber Co., circa 1903.

Fifteen thousand barrels of flour were destroyed on March 5, 1914, when North Yakima Milling Co. burned in spectacular blaze.

Newer Helliesen Lumber Co. buildings went up in flames on
April 19, 1914.

As automobiles became more common, city residents were able to explore the country around them, both near and far. This is the picnic ground at Naches City.

A stop for lunch along the road near Cowiche, July, 1915.

Washing dishes after the Tillicum Club picnic in the Wenas, June, 1915.

Camp site at Soda Springs, a quicker destination by car than it had been by livery when it was a four-to-six hour ride.

Crawford's Band, 1913 Fair.

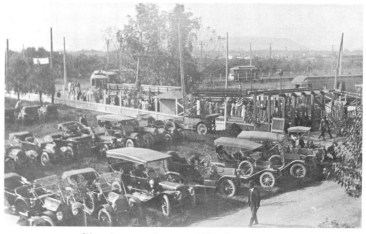

Street car entrance, 1913 State Fair.

Autos at 1913 State Fair.

Women's Building, State Fair.

Yakima Avenue beflagged for Fair.

Modern Woodmen provide varying facilities.

The rustic bridge at Sumac Park.

Between North Yakima and Moxee was Sumac Park,
a favorite picnic ground.

Breakfast in camp, August 1913.

Late evening, Mill Creek camp, 1913.

Several families camped together at Soda Springs.

Naches Avenue, always beautiful, as it appeared,
south from A Street, on January 1, 1915.

On snowy New Year's Day in 1915, Naches Avenue
was quiet and white, north from A Street.

Thirty-three miles
into the Wenas for
this 1912 picnic.

A long walk through the Wenas woods after lunch.

An early highway.

Apple Day, April 5, 1913, provided the theme for men's store window display. Lower right, Frank Lanterman's radio-phonograph department at the Emporium. Below, his delivery wagon.

A three-car caravan sets out for Portland in August, 1916.

Canvas converts car into a tent on Portland excursion.

Mitchell's Point, Columbia River Highway, summer 1916.

"Kitchen and dining room" for Mr. and Mrs. Lanterman.

Along the Naches River, July 2, 1916.

About face! Ready for hiking trip, 1916.

Autos bring trouble as well as freedom to roam!

Canyon near Soda Springs, 1916.

Naches Road at
Rock Creek, 1915.

Fishing in Tieton area, 1918.

Picnic gathering, August 1915.

Fisherwomen pose.

This board road led to an Oregon beach.

Clam digging, summer 1918.

Sunset Beach camping site, summer 1918.

The second St. Elizabeth Hospital, this building received its first patient in August, 1892. The hospital, at Fourth and E Streets, grew within a ten-year period to a 65-bed capacity, and in the early 1900s handled many typhoid fever cases. The Sisters of Providence had started the hospital in 1891, in response to a request by the U.S. Reclamation Service which sought care for government employes in the area.

On April 13, 1913, the cornerstone was laid for the new St. Elizabeth Hospital on Ninth Avenue, and on January 1, 1914, the hospital admitted its first patient, "a poor Indian," according to church history. "In the new hospital, Yakima's citizens showed a tangible interest . . . furnished rooms, embellished the chapel, donated statues, and helped to meet interest obligations."

602. St. Elizabeth's Hospital, No. Yakima, Wash.

From the new hospital chimney, this was the view northwest across Tenth and Eleventh Avenues. The triangular park formed by the bend in Yakima Avenue is right center.

A closer view from the hospital chimney shows the site of **Portia Park** and Summit View (later Roosevelt) school at right center.

The growing west side of North Yakima appears in this picture taken toward the northeast. Columbia School is right center.

Southwest from the hospital lay the open fields stretching **toward** Ahtanum ridge.

On Armistice Day, November 11, 1918, Yakima Avenue was clogged with hundreds of citizens who gathered to celebrate the end of World War I. Riding in the open car lower left were Mr. and Mrs. Lee Sheeley.

Yakima Federal Savings and Loan Association was at 114 East Yakima Avenue, just west of its present location, in this 1921 view. The association had its offices here for about 35 years.

# WAPATO

Once the nucleus of a community called Simcoe, Wapato was renamed in 1903, and two years later was laid out by Alexander McCredy. He and George S. Rankin formed the Wapato Development Co. which dedicated the townsite on July 21, 1905.

Wapato Central School, early 1900s.

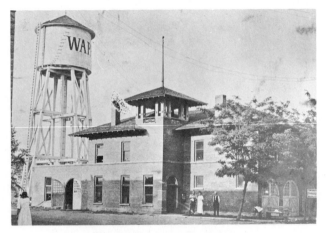

City hall was built in 1908.

Wapato Avenue looking south, 1910.

Hotel Wapato was built in 1907.

Interior, Wapato Trading Company.

Wapato Presbyterian Church.

Blacksmith shop interior, Wapato.

Joe Yolo in Winton 6, 1915 state fair races.

Catholic Church, Wapato.

Wapato's main street, 1906.

Wapato depot, 1906.

Livery, feed stable.

Wapato elementary school, 1904.

# TOPPENISH

First Avenue was Fort Road when these frame buildings lined it in the early 1900s. After they burned, brick ones replaced them.

Old high school, Toppenish.

The old passenger station in Toppenish later became the freight depot.

Under construction in 1908 was the Episcopal Church, adjacent to the Lincoln School.

Identical to the Lincoln School, the Garfield School was being completed in 1908.

A lovely balcony graced the Hotel Toppenish, built in 1907.

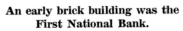

An early brick building was the First National Bank.

From Horse Shoe Bar at right, South Division Street as it was in 1913.

Gilbert Co. catered to immigrants who came during land boom. McLean Transfer owned wagon in picture.

The Central Bank Building, Toppenish, 1913.

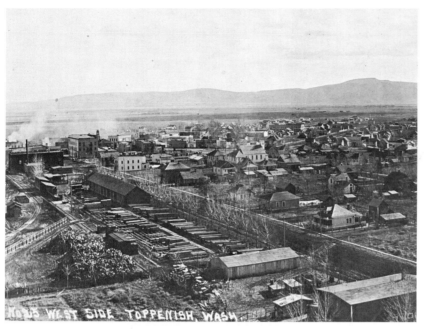

West side of Toppenish, 1912.

Indian horses are corralled at Toppenish, May 1912.

The Toppenish Commercial Club inspected the Yakima Indian
Reservation canal near the outlet of the Yakima River in 1911.

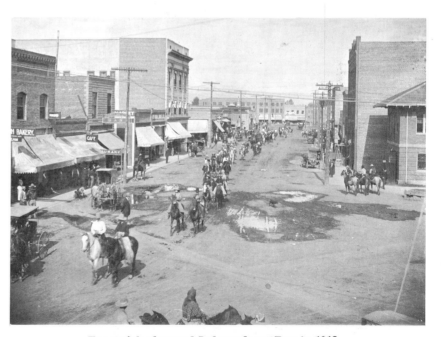

Toppenish observed Independence Day in 1913
with a parade on Toppenish Avenue.

# ZILLAH

In 1912, Zillah was a small town of approximately 400 persons, and was the center of a fruit raising district, with one half of the entire harvest of Yakima County fruit coming from Zillah. Orchards, vineyards and hop fields yielded major crops in the growing area.

Zillah public school, 1912.

Business block, 1911.

OWR and N depot, Zillah, with motor car.

Northern Pacific depot, after 1912.

First Christian Church, circa 1911.

Sunnyside canal intake on Yakima River, near Zillah.

# GRANGER

Liberty School, early 1900s.

Granger jail, 1910.

Granger in 1903 had a post office, left, a grocery store, a hotel, a pump in the middle of the street, and school and dance hall in building at right.

July, 1913, baseball game saw Granger girls defeat fat men!

Old hotel at Alfalfa.

Granger Livery and Feed Co.

# SUNNYSIDE

"The insatiable courage and drive of the pioneer settler and his family" contributed much to the success of Sunnyside, according to Roscoe Sheller. His family settled there after the Progressive Brethren Church purchased the townsite to build a Christian Cooperative Community. The town was incorporated in 1902, as it appears here.

Walter N. Granger had laid out Sunnyside commenting that "as I gazed on the scene, I then and there resolved that a city should some day be built at the base of the mountain, for the site was ideal." Sunnyside prospered. Sixth Street looking east around 1910, left.

Edison Street, main shopping block in Sunnyside, circa 1910.

Grand-View Heights lay beyond Oregon-Washington Railroad and
Navigation depot, circa 1911.

Sunnyside High School under construction, 1910.

Public Library, built 1911.

Beyond downtown, with Baraca Building, Federated Church,
was Harrison Hill.

Far left, L. B. George Department Store; left, Sunnyside Bank.

Looking north on Sixth Street toward intersection with Edison, circa 1910.

East side of Sixth Street, between alley, present Giffen Building.

Hitchcock Building housed Sun, 1907.

North on Sixth Street, near Franklin, circa 1905.

The three-story Sunnyside Hotel was center of town in this 1899 Sunnyside view.

Crowds waited in vain at depot in February, 1906, as train bringing dignitaries mired in mud before it reached town.

Two-story Odd Fellows Building dominated 1907 view of Sunnyside, hotel to left center.

The Washington School on Factory Road, three miles east of Sunnyside, early 1900s.

James Henderson, left, was proprietor of Henderson's
Drug Store, photographed 1907. Right, J. T. Baird.

Outlook store and hall, 1913.

# GRANDVIEW

Because the domes of Mt. Adams and Mt. Rainier and the broad expanse of the Yakima Valley presented a "grand view," that name was chosen for the townsite which was opened in 1906 and incorporated in 1909. The Northern Pacific depot was erected in 1912.

N.P. PASSENGER STATION
GRANDVIEW, WASH.

The Grandview depot of the Oregon-Washington Railroad and Navigation Co. opened on March 22, 1911, when the big excursion from Walla Walla to Yakima marked the opening of the line, later known as the North Coast Railroad.

Grandview, 1906.

Grandview, 1911.

Division and South Second Streets, 1911.

Grandview's business section, looking from southeast, 1911.

Grandview's first school, built 1907.

Bethany Presbyterian Church, built 1905, moved to town 1908.

First Methodist Church, erected in 1909.

The old Central Hotel in Grandview.

The Free Methodist Church, built 1908.

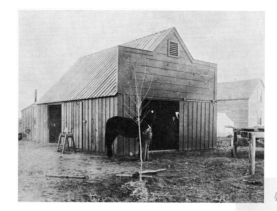

Far left, Grandview's first bakery; left, first blacksmith shop.

The first store in Grandview.

Mrs. A. E. Sykes from Everett built the town's first building in 1906, served as postmistress downstairs, rented lodgings upstairs.

The first bank in Grandview.

Marvin Martin's Livery Stable.

# MABTON

NO-10-MAIN STREET-MABTON-WASH,

In the early 1900s Mabton was an important railroad stop, with freight put off there for other valley communities. B Street toward the east had a two-story brick building, several frame ones.

Mabton's Main Street in 1910 showed a growing town, which had done much rebuilding after an early and disastrous fire had swept many buildings along the tracks as well as the town's one live tree.

A later picture of B Street, circa 1911, reveals a street light, additional brick buildings.

Another block of B Street, Mabton's business section, circa 1907.

Mabton's High School was dedicated
on Oct. 20, 1911, at special ceremonies.

The Mabton Hotel, circa 1910.

In the great flood of 1906, only the railings
of the Mabton bridge remained above water.

This store on Main Street offered
a general variety of merchandise.

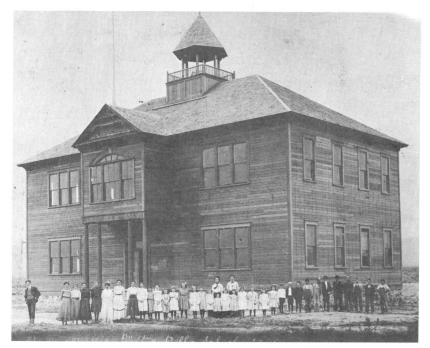

Mabton Public School, 1905.

# PROSSER

**Prosser's Sixth Street, 1907.**

**Prosser High School, 1907.**

**Prosser Hotel, Sixth Street and Meade Avenue, circa 1911.**

**Riverview School, circa 1907.**

Prosser Falls and Rapids, with old wooden flume which washed out in flood.

Prosser dam, built 1906, against bridge, Horse Heaven Hills.

The Sixth Street wagon bridge opened for traffic two weeks before 1906 flood, was protected by tons of rock on floor.

River and falls at Prosser.

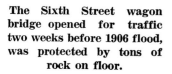

Sprinkler used to wet down dusty streets, 1907.

Steel bridge built in 1911 replaced wooden bridge washed out in flood.

The Victor, bakery and restaurant on Bennett Avenue, 1902.

Patriotic display for Chautauqua program, 1914, Crescent Clothing window.

Yakima River at flood stage, November, 1906.

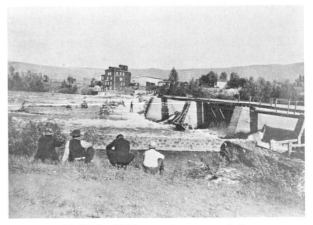

Built in 1906 was dam near falls.

Ice Combined Harvester, 1915.

Independence Day 1905 was observed with this parade on Sixth near Meade Avenue in Prosser.

A bird's eye view of Prosser, wheat country focus, in 1907.

A promotion in the summer of 1907 at the Crescent Clothing and Kash-Savin Store in Prosser.

West of town, the Benton County Fair racetrack, in 1907.

Panoramic view of threshing and heading operation in wheat country near Prosser, in 1914.

Horse Heaven country threshing outfit near Prosser.

Combine harvester, Horse Heaven country, 1907.

# KENNEWICK

Kennewick's origins lie in the building of a railroad bridge across the river before the turn of the century, but not until its third platting by the Northern Pacific Railway in 1902 did the town become firmly established. Then a land rush developed and settlers flocked to the area with resultant prosperity.

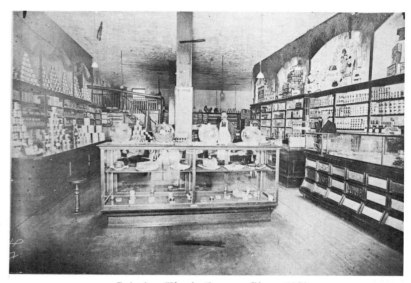

**Interior, King's Grocery Store, 1909.**

**Homestead, Kennewick, 1909.**

**Kennewick Avenue, east toward Washington Street, city hall at left.**

**Washington School in Kennewick.**

The Courier Office on
Kennewick Ave., 1912.

**Port of Kennewick opens, 1915,
with special cruise to ocean.**

**King's store, Washington St. and
Kennewick Ave., 1905.**

**Sagebrush was gathered for Thanksgiving
dinner fuel by homesteading family.**

A Busy street in Kennewick Wash. in 1906.

Harvest in the Horse Heaven Hills was destination
of three combines in Kennewick, 1906.

**Kennewick Avenue, 1908.**

Kennewick Ave —

# PASCO

Pasco's Christian Church, built 1915.

A road through sagebrush leads to early-day Pasco.

After successful rabbit hunt, Pasco.

Mr. and Mrs. Joe Stark in buggy, 1910.

Clark Street, looking north from Fifth Street,
Pasco, 1912.

Pasco Hotel lobby, 1915.

Being loaded for delivery from Pasco to Coulee City in 1905 was this stack of 100,000 wheat sacks.

Villard Hotel, "modernly equipped," helped to make Pasco a "rendezvous for commercial travelers" who found town convenient base for covering surrounding territory.

Pasco's early-day depot.

Pasco Hardware Co.
interior, 1910.

Pasco Flour Mill.

Pasco Hardware Co.
delivery rig, 1914.

Pasco Reclamation Co. pumping plant on Snake River had footings 22 feet below surface, four-feet thick walls.

Fredrick Stimson, founder, at his Crescent Drug Store, Fourth Ave. and Lewis St., 1910.